GET GOING.

Riley Temple

Get Going.
ISBN 978-1-5136-1405-2

Written by Riley Temple

Published in the United States of America by
Quiddity, Inc.
3760 Market Street NE #127
Salem, Oregon
97301

This book was produced in collaboration with
TheGoingGoods.com

DEDICATION.

For the adventure-crazed who baffle, astound, and inspire.

Thanks to the fam for
living brave, giving big, and having fun.
You've encouraged me to be brave and face my fears.

And to my Spark. You know.

YO.

You inspire me.
You just picked up a book about backpacking the world.
That tells me a lot about you.

It tells me:
You are curious.
You are driven.
You listen to your own voice.
You are courageous.
You are open.
You are ready to get going.

I'm inspired by you being you.

I WROTE THIS BECAUSE.

1. This world is full of inspiration which can be overwhelming. With so many people doing amazing things sometimes its hard to decide what amazing things you want to do. This book was written to help you get going.

2. Friends asked for it. This document was adapted and expanded from a letter to a good friend planning a trip to Southeast Asia. Then others wanted a copy. I love writing, so I turned that letter it into this book.

I'm Riley Temple, writer and traveler. You've spent enough time being amazed at other people's decisions, it's time to inspire yourself, it's your time to get going.

Being inspired to get going has led me
around the world and back.

THESE ARE SOME TRIPS I'VE TAKEN IN MY 19 YEARS.

- Traveled with a group of musicians while teaching English in western Turkey at 15.
- Backpacked the world for nine months with my family at the age of 16.
- Couch surfed my way around the Bay Area immediately after highschool.
- Founded a VC-funded Financial Education Corporation for Millenials at 18 in Silicon Valley.
- Went to Thailand as a brand ambassador for a travel start-up at 19.
- Wrote this on a plane to the Dominican Republic.

I hope this book inspires you to get going, too.

Before every section break I leave a blank page.

This space is for you to **fill.**

Notes, quotes, drawings, itineraries, ideas - it's all yours.

Have fun making this book your own.

WHAT YOU'RE GETTING YOURSELF INTO.

"The jump is so frightening between
where I am and where I want to be,
but because of all I may become, I
will close my eyes and leap."

\- Mary Anne Radmacher

@rileytemp

WHAT YOU'RE GETTING YOURSELF INTO.

trav·el
/ˈtravəl/
verb

To go on a trip or journey: to go to a place and especially one that is far away.

Travel is not a "one size fits all" glove. There are many ways to explore this planet, and lately I've noticed a big pull toward the backpacker lifestyle. The raw, spontaneous, volunteer-filled, bold and bodacious way of sight searching is picking up steam. People are strapping on backpacks instead of dragging suitcases. They are trading pool-side service for local exploration.

This is what I'd like to help you do.

When asked, "Why do you love travel?" I could easily list the stories, friends, food, and places I have experienced worldwide, and even after that impromptu story sesh, you still wouldn't see the full impact it has had on me.

I want you to know that while you travel you're not only discovering the world, you're also discovering yourself. You get to experience such diverse cultures, people, and customs; they change your perspective and that changes you.

This is why I recommend travel to anyone who is questioning themselves. It's hard to change perspectives when everything stays the same, to expand who you are and what you think. I often feel stuck and directionless when home, but when I'm on the road I find the direction I'm after. It's what drives me.

I think of it like this.

When it comes to self-discovery, we're each like an object in a dark room waiting to be revealed. Each experience in life turns on a light around us and slowly we start seeing the shape, color, and texture of the object, which is us.

As the room gets brighter and brighter, we are able to see the context of that object - where it sits, what surrounds it, how it looks compared to its surroundings. Soon we start looking for ways and places it can be used.

Through that experience, you and I can start seeing what we can do, how we bring value, and where we sit in this room we call the world.

There's nothing like travel to light you up.

PACKS AND GEAR.

"I haven't been everywhere,
but it's on my list."
- Susan Sontag

PACKS AND GEAR.

I traveled nine months around the world out of one backpack and a guitar case. Twenty minutes of packing, I could be mobile and onto the next town. My home, and all I owned, was on my back, and I loved it.

The turtle life changed me.

It's a liberating feeling having your life on your back. It changed my perspective of what's really necessary and introduced me to the minimalistic lifestyle that's trending now.

I will admit, at first, I packed wayyyy too much. My second trip, I packed wayy too much. My third, I packed too much. And even now, I still find myself leaving things behind while on the road.

High quality, low quantity.

That's my biggest tip for packing. When it comes to essentials, buy the best. When it comes to replaceables, the disposables, you can buy them on the road, often at a better price.

You'll find your own way through this process and as you begin taking trips you'll determine your own "must-haves" and "do-withouts."

MY PACK LIST.

This is what I packed on my last Thailand trip. I've added some suggestions for girls. Also, keep in mind I pack to carry-on. I don't want to worry about losing checked bags so I keep everything on me. This may not be your style. Try all your options out, but I will let you know – keeping your bags with you is the way to go.

Note* This may look like a long list but it packs small.

Documents:

- ☐ Current Passport. You should probably have this:) Your passport should be at least eight months from expiration, and have 5+ blank pages for entry and exit stamps.
- ☐ 5 - photocopies of your passport. For yourself, to share with your travel partners, and to leave at home with family.
- ☐ 3 to 5 - passport photos. Some countries require these for you to receive your visa.
- ☐ Travelers and Medical Insurance card
- ☐ Emergency Contact Info
- ☐ Information regarding any prescribed medication

Money:

- ☐ 2 - Debit cards. One for daily use, one as back-up in case of loss.
- ☐ Wallet, money clip, or pouch for daily cash and coin
- ☐ Incognito pouch to hide reserve cash and secondary debit card (similar to a money hidden under clothing)
- ☐ $50 USD. This is your just in case stash. Just about every country in the world exchanges US currency.

Bags:

- ☐ Main backpack. 41L w/ padded shoulder straps, internal frame, hip support, and lots of inner and outer pockets.
- ☐ Electronics bag. As to what you bring, make sure it is padded and relatively hard to get into.
- ☐ Day pack. Folds up very small, quick drying, great for laundry. Drawstring bags are always solid options here.
- ☐ Fanny pack. Rad for keeping documents within reach while in transit and for day adventures where a backpack seems a bit bulky.

Clothes:

Keep in mind the time of year and climate you're headed into. This will be the biggest influence on your clothing choices. This list is from my last trip to Thailand.

- ☐ 2 - T-Shirts
- ☐ 2 - Tanks (or lightweight tops)
- ☐ Long sleeve shirt, even in tropical spots (saves you from bugs and the sun, if burnt)
- ☐ Flannel/sweater/fleece (or other lighter layer)
- ☐ Button-down shirt (Don't know when you'll need to get a lil' fancy. Girls, you can always rock a sundress.)
- ☐ Lightweight rain jacket or rain poncho
- ☐ 2 - Shorts
- ☐ 2 - Pants. I pack one pair of jeans, but keep in mind they do not dry quickly and can be very bulky.
- ☐ Bathing suit. (Girls! I know you dig options here. Maybe 2 suits you can mix and match tops and bottoms?)
- ☐ Girls! A dress that doubles as a swimsuit cover or Sarong, which you can buy on the road.
- ☐ 5 - Pairs of socks. Mix and match high and low cut. Clean dry socks might be your best friends on the road.
- ☐ 5 - Pairs of underwear. Your choice what type. Just think breathability, comfort, quick-dry.
- ☐ Girls! One sports bra and two regular bras (So say the girl travelers anyway).
- ☐ Fabric belt (great for a variety of things)
- ☐ Hats. Ballcaps to bucket hats, fedoras to fezzes - find your style and bring one along.

Shoes:

- ☐ Everyday - You'll be putting miles on these so it is uber important to find a comfy and walkable shoe for yourself. I travel with Converse. These may change pending on what you'd consider an "everyday" shoe. I've yet to travel with anything else, so do your research if canvas and rubber chucks don't float your fancy. Plus, Converse go with just about everything and are purchasable worldwide. Just sayin.'

- ☐ Water/Hiking - Nike Frees, or any lightweight mesh shoe, are perfect for hiking/water adventures. They pack nicely, dry quickly in the sun, are machine washable (if they smell a tad funky), and can be used for workout shoes (if you're into that kinda stuff).

- ☐ Flip flops - Great for the beach, grody hostel showers, or casually lounging around your hostel or hotel.

 Pro tip: Bring some clothes you don't mind leaving behind (or donating!). Clear up some room in your pack so you can purchase rad local clothing.

I still get comments on a sweet alpaca sweater I copped in Peru, boots from Spain, elephant tank from Thailand, and board shorts from Australia (which are ripped to shreds now:/).

Here are some of those replaceables I mentioned before. I'll usually start out with these and buy more on the road if needed, but if I leave without something on the list, I don't stress. I can pick it up along the way. Just make sure you have them so you're ready for just about anything.

Toiletries:

No liquids over four ounces and no aerosols if you're carrying on.

- ☐ Toiletries Bag
- ☐ Travel Shampoo and/or bodywash
- ☐ Quick-drying travel towel (make sure it packs well)
- ☐ Toothbrush + (TSA approved) toothpaste
- ☐ Dental floss (many uses for this)
- ☐ Chapstick (Being in transit dries my lips out like crazy)
- ☐ Small nail clippers
- ☐ Earplugs
- ☐ Deodorant
- ☐ Little perfume/cologne (mask your smell with a little more smell)

Medical whatnots:

- ☐ Any doctor prescribed medications you may take (keep your pills in your prescription bottle when going through airport security)
- ☐ Basic first aid kit, including: Band-aids, hydrocortisone cream, sanitizing/wet-wipes, small travel-safe tweezers, anti-bacterial cream, several feet of gauze, cotton swabs
- ☐ Benadryl Pills (works for allergies and sleep aid)
- ☐ Ibuprofen
- ☐ Dramamine
- ☐ Hand sanitizer (TSA approved size)
- ☐ Contraceptives (relative to gender)

- ☐ Sunscreen
- ☐ Bugspray

Tech:

- ☐ Cellphone and charger
- ☐ Surgebar
- ☐ Headlamp
- ☐ Universal outlet plug
- ☐ Headphones
- ☐ Laptop and charger
- ☐ Camera
- ☐ 2 - SD memory cards (32 and 64 gig)
- ☐ 2 - Batteries for camera and a charging port
- ☐ GoPro camera (and all its toys and cables)
- ☐ 1 terabyte hard drive. Running out of storage space sucks on the road.

Rando necessities:

- ☐ Notebook (for budgeting, notes, info to remember, etc.)
- ☐ Journal (when you're feeling inspired)
- ☐ Pocket sketch pad
- ☐ Pens and pencils
- ☐ Compression packing bags
- ☐ Ziplock bags
- ☐ Travel-ready sewing kit
- ☐ 10' of multipurpose rope
- ☐ 5 - Carabiners (3 large, 2 small)
- ☐ TSA approved combination luggage lock
- ☐ Small roll of Duct Tape

- ☐ Bic sized Lighter or waterproof matches
- ☐ TSA approved multi-tool. Don't be too bummed if its confiscated by security.
- ☐ Deck of cards (a fun way to meet people and learn new games from around the world)
- ☐ Travel Hammock (makes everywhere nappable)

Optionals:

There will be lulls in the action. Find ways to keep yourself and others entertained on the road. Try bringing something you're not good at and learn on the road - that's how I picked up playing the guitar.

- ☐ Guitar or Ukulele (Music is a universally understood language; this is my conversation catalyst of choice.)
- ☐ Hacky Sack
- ☐ A book
- ☐ Suduko, crossword puzzles, wordfinds, etc.

PACKING TIPS.

Use compression bags.

These bad boys will save you a lot of room. Plus after sealing them shut, your clothes are safe from spontaneous rain storms, a bag drop in the ocean, or any other catastrophic event involving water and mud.

 Pro tip: Want to make the most of that space? **Roll those clothes.** I've tried just about every tactic to squeeze as much as I can into a backpack. It may not keep the clothes wrinkle free, but I have a feeling no one is going to call you out on it.

Leave some room.

Somehow, someway, you will fill your bag to its capacity - especially on the first trip. Plan on bringing anything back from your adventures? Then plan on leaving something behind, or just leave some room.

Strap it when things get nasty.

When shoes, shorts, and shirts get sandy, wet, and smelly you don't want to stick that stuff back in your pack along with your other decent clothing. Use a carabiner or tie that grungy gear to the outside of your main pack so it can dry and not taint the rest of your stuff.

Ziplock your liquids.

When you open your toiletries bag to find toothpaste squished and smeared over everything <

Throw spill-prone liquids in ziplock bags to keep that fresh paste in the tube.

Wear your bulkiest shoes in transit to save space in your bag.

But if your bulkiest shoes are still wet and caked from your muddy jungle adventures, resort back to the "Strap it when things get nasty" tip. When my converse are soaked, putting even more distance on them while carrying my pack is just asking for blisters. Clean those shoes off, let them dry on the outside of your bag, and rock your next best option (I'd reach for my Frees).

INTERNET AND CELLULAR PLANS.

'Cause your fam and friends want to be in the loop.

INTERNET AND CELLULAR PLANS.

Maslow's hierarchy of needs just got a little bigger:

Internet is the sidekick and villain of this story. A necessary evil.

Most of the time I find myself hopping from WiFi to WiFi in lobbies, coffee houses, and restaurants. You will, too. It helps you book lodging, communicate with friends, find the best restaurants, make travel reservations, and check out nearby adventures.

A strong WiFi connection aids in your exploration - but it also distracts. Some of the most frustrating times are spent finding good WiFi. Places will say they have it, but when you hop on - nothing. Or maybe it will load part of a page - just enough to get your hopes up and then disappoint, leaving you high and dry when booking.

Internet won't always be available; plan accordingly.

When you find solid WiFi make the most of it.

Here's how:

- Take screenshots of your bookings (lodging names, addresses, check-in/out times, etc.). Don't count on your email browser to always load your booking confirmation.
- Screenshot maps you feel you may need that day.
- Record any needed phone numbers just in case internet communication isn't available.
- Complete necessary tasks first - you never know when WiFi will give out. Do what you need to get done, then continue with your casual internet browsing.
- Load wanted documents/books, videos, music for offline use - when you're wanting to jam, you don't want a lack of internet to get in the way.

 Pro tip: Keep your documents, screenshots, and other information organized by immediately labeling and creating proper files so you can quickly find them later. The guessing game isn't fun to play when vital info is needed asap.

Batteries die. Notepads don't. If something is essential to getting you where you need to go - write it down on a piece of paper you can access later. Pump out what you know will help you have a successful day, then enjoy where you are.

Internet on the road is your tool **for** exploration –
don't let it distract you **from** exploration.

This is something I remind myself everyday - at home and on the road.
Look at where you are. Enjoy it. Take it in. It beats social media any day.

Use the internet with moderation,
then take hold of your day.

CELLULAR PLANS.

I'd highly recommend having a phone number for local communication
wherever you are traveling. Check with your current service provider for
any international plans – **do not** assume you're covered internationally for
data, text, and minutes.

An $800 phone bill for international usage
is not a fun thing to come home to.

Do your homework, but if you want to play it safe you can go two routes:

1. Prepaid SIM card
2. Local SIM card

For the longest time, I would buy an international SIM card in the states
with pre-loaded minutes, texts, and data. There's value in doing it, because
some airports don't have publicly accessible WiFi. By arriving with a SIM
card, I had a way of communicating with lodging providers and scheduled
transportation services.

Trouble is, I faced a consistent issue. I would quickly run out of data/ minutes, and cellular connection usually wasn't as strong as it was for the locals.

Last trip I took to Thailand, a friend showed me an alternative route: Buy the SIM there.

Even though it may be a hassle figuring out which provider and plan to go with, it makes up for it on the backend. You get a local number, the plan uses the strongest available cell connection, and you can upgrade your cell/data for a fraction of the cost in comparison to international providers (my friend upgraded to an unlimited data plan in Thailand for 400 Thai Baht ~ $12 USD).

It'll be more expensive to make international calls, but if you save those minutes through internet-supported communication, you'll come out on top.

To use these SIM cards:

Either bring an unlocked phone capable of taking other providers' SIM cards, or buy a cheap burn phone there.

OTHER FORMAL STUFF.

Hoops to jump through
before you hop in the
plane and go.

OTHER FORMAL STUFF.

If you're a U.S. citizen, sneak a peek at www.state.gov/travel/. It's your source for current information on passports, visas, international emergencies, resources, and travel prep provided by the U.S. government.

TRAVELERS INSURANCE.

As a traveler, you have a decision to make. Will you buy traveler's insurance or not? It's a way to cover the possible "ifs" of a trip.

I make sure to have my ifs, ands, and butt covered.
'Cause you never know.

It's nice to be covered financially if you encounter any health, political, travel delays, theft, and/or natural disasters. Those circumstances can definitely throw your budget off. Having another wallet to reach into for a little help when things take a turn gives you solid peace of mind.

Find an insurance provider and plan that works best for your trip and decide for or against the protection.

It's not as expensive as you'd think.
Definitely worth scoping out.

STARTING HEALTHY.

A question I am asked a lot is, "How did you prep for the possibility of being sick?"

I wish I could throw an M.D. next to my name, but the amount of school it'd take me to earn it would most likely send me to the doctor. This information is pulled from my personal experience, and if you have any concern for your own health before and during your trip, chat up a real doctor.

Yes, unfortunately this is something you have to really consider, but the amount of prep is again a decision you need to make.

The choice involves vaccinations. Some countries require specific vaccinations before entering as well - so there's a little more homework for ya. Should you load up on shots/pills? Avoid high-risk areas? Get the minimum vaccinations required to enter said country?

One way to make this decision easier is to get a titer test.

"A titer (TIGHT er) test is a test that detects the presence and amount of antibodies within a person's blood."
(Source Healthline.com)

With this test you can see what your body is most susceptible to. Knowing this info will aid in your decision about what vaccinations to get.

Your body, your choice.

STAYING HEALTHY ON THE ROAD.

It makes it really hard to fully enjoy a location when your body is out of sync. Getting sick is a reality for most frequent travelers, so defend yourself by knowing how to avoid it, and if you've been compromised, combat the germy world of a backpacker. Here are your tools to fight it:

First aid kit.
You may be getting on and off the struggle bus of health. Having a first aid kit to speed the transition is a must for any traveler.

Organic apple cider vinegar.
Upset stomach after eating something sketchy? Chase it with apple cider vinegar. Poison Oak/Ivy rash? Apple cider vinegar. Stuffy nose? ACV.

Apple cider vinegar has an incredible amount of uses, not only for a fresh salad, but to smooth the day-to-day health of a travel backpacker. The acids in apple cider vinegar when consumed, orally or topically, alkalize the body, killing viruses or bacteria that may be trying to grow.

I'd highly recommend scoping out the many ways to make the most of apple cider vinegar and purchase a small bottle on the road. It saved me from countless amounts of sick seshes.

Motion sickness relief.
Dramamine is an over-the-counter drug for anti-vomiting and nausea. Its rad, buttttt -

I was told by a captain of a major cruise line that an apple does the trick as well. I was skeptical at first, but did a little research. Here's what I found:

An apple contains pectin, a compound that neutralizes your stomach acid which, in turn, prevents motion sickness. Between the pectin and the natural sugars, which also act to settle the stomach, you've got a rad little remedy to stop reliving your last meal via a curvy bus ride through the mountains of Peru.

Steve, the boat captain, said he's seen grannies practically puking out their dentures - but after a few bites on an apple, they were back playing shuffleboard with the gramps like champs.

Shoutout to Captain Steve for the knowledge bomb and to topnaturalremedies.net for the sciencey stuff to validate!

Biggest tip I can recommend if you are sick on the road:

Take your time to recover.

By playing it off like nothing is happening, you'll drag it out. If you travel sick, your body will have a tougher time getting rid of whatever is bogging you down. Take your time to get well. Adventures aren't as fun when you pretend to be okay between coughs and wheezes.

It isn't a good time - I've tried it.

Your time is valuable, your body is valuable. Respect both by allowing yourself to fully recover.

Sideline yourself, hydrate, rest, and hit the road again when you've gained sobriety from your sickness.

A constant reminder to myself: Lows make the highs that much better - the discipline is enjoying the **whole** process. Laughing at yourself, even in the lowest of lows, is the sign of an experienced traveler.

POWER OF ATTORNEY.

Not a fun conversation, but a necessary one. Who speaks on your behalf if something goes down?

Signing a Power of Attorney gives someone you trust the power to make financial and medical decisions if necessary. Powerofattorney.com will get you those free documents. Scope it.

VISAS.

Visas vary from country to country and they change depending on the country you're from.

What is a visa?

vi·sa
/ˈvēzə/
noun

A visa is an endorsement on a passport indicating that the holder is allowed to enter, leave, or stay for a specific period of time in a country.

Unfortunately, most countries don't gift those endorsements out freely. Visas cost money at the front, and occasionally on the backend as well. If you're considering taking a trip to a country, scope out the visa requirements and what it'll cost you to cross borders.

Again, www.state.gov/travel/ will give you the visa information needed to budget accordingly.

Note* A majority of countries require proof of exit. When you arrive, you need to show proof that you have booked transportation out of the country.

I like to keep an open itinerary –
governments aren't keen on this type of traveling.

They want to know where you've been, where you'll be, and where you're headed. This kind of fizzles out the spontaneous backpacker's plans to not have plans. There are ways around this.

Showing proof of exit transportation:

Most countries require proof of exit and expect you to show it to them. This is tough when you go out of your way not to have an itinerary, but necessary if continuing to travel is on your agenda.

However, this is an easy issue to solve. You may not have an exact departure date set, but as long as you're aware of the time frame you have in that country, you can choose a date that might work and do this:

Screenshot (or print out) the transportation info confirmation screen just **before** you purchase.

It needs to be easy to read and relatively true to the date and location you'll be leaving the country. You want the document to relfect your intention to leave on time.

Most transportation is easily purchased online so the pre-order confirmation screen should be easy to capture.

If you are using local transportation with no online presence, the best you can do is write down all the information you can gather, as well as the name of the service provider. This is a way to show you respect the country you're in and still travel loose. Just make sure to take off before that visa expires!

MY FIRST TRIP: STORYTIME.

Sophomore year I was invited on my first international experience. Not only that, but I got to travel with a group of musicians up and down the west coast of Turkey teaching English through music. It was a pretty rad invitation to receive.

Note*: This was a separate trip from my "No-Go-Moe" trip I mention later in the book.

I was psyched. Nervous, but psyched. *this is a theme.

I was also trusting because the person leading the trip had a personal connection to a local founder of an English school who would guide us. So things were laid out for us. I just needed the money.

Several months of odd jobs later I had the chunk of change I needed to hit the road. Once that bank account hit the mark, I remember thinking to myself, "Well shit, now I really have to do this."

I mean, Turkey? At the time it wouldn't even make my top ten for the most desirable countries to visit. But I had an opportunity, a group to travel with, a plan laid out for me, a guitar, and an itch to say yes.

So I did.

I left for Turkey with a group of people I hardly knew, trusting a concept that felt more foreign than the country I was flying to. I'd been playing guitar for maybe three months, so it felt awkward to be considered a musician, let alone teaching English through music.

Two feelings persist when I began saying yes to the unknown, and they still show up when I say yes to something I'm clueless about:

Nervousness and Excitement.

These feelings took over. I couldn't stop my mind from racing between scenarios: "What if they find out I have no clue what I'm doing with this instrument?" "What if my English ain't no good and I teach these kids some absurd interpretation of my half-developed 15-year-old west coast jargon?"

My mind wouldn't stop. The night before I left I couldn't sleep for fear of being found out that I was a phony leech tagging along to this musically inclined troop. I took my fears with me to the airport and then felt them dissolve as I met my fellow travelers. Smiles, laughter, thankfulness that I'd shown up in service, and finally...

Excitement.
All of which made my nervousness irrelevant.

I then realized what got me out of bed at 2 a.m. for that first flight. It was the excitement of the unknown, and that excitement outweighed any nervousness I still had. I was left with a long list of "What if?" questions, and if I had let this opportunity pass I would have never been able to explore the answers.

And I wanted answers.

That, and several months of work, prep, and sleepless nights, gave the subtle nudge for me to get going. More on the outcome of my first trip later in the book.

You don't score a touchdown by only taking the ball to the 10-yard line. I had ten more yards and a flight to Turkey to go.

KEEPING TO A BUDGET.

Tools and tips
to help.

KEEPING TO A BUDGET.

There are a lot of things to consider when budgeting a trip. Things like:

- Where are you going?
- Where do you want to stay?
- What do you want to do?
- How are you going to get around?
- Souvenirs?

But the overarching question for all the above is:

What is your comfort level?

Pretty plain to see if you prefer the posh lifestyle it'll cost you. But if hostel living and local food floats your fancy, you'll be sitting in a bit comfier space financially.

How I self-funded my last Thailand trip and what it cost me:

Only two months of work gave me enough money to take the trip. In total, I spent $1,300 for 22 days of travel which did not include the flight.

Even that was a tad spendy as I was frequently moving between cities, which eats away at the budget quickly.

Remember, transportation is going to be your biggest expense so make sure you plan accordingly.

If you remain in one place for a while you're going to save some money. Being on the move has its hidden expenses, not only because of the transportation cost itself, but pricing fluctuates and budgeting is harder to predict.

The more you move the more you spend.

The backpacker lifestyle runs me about $40 dollars a day for lodging, food, and transportation, although I shoot for about $30/day. That's $900 - $1,200 per month (not including the flight).

Daily budgeting is a balancing act.

Some days you'll overspend, others you'll underspend.

Price ranges fluctuate as the day progresses and money is spent. Budgeting is about balance and determining your priorities that day. A little extra on dinner or upgrade to a private room in your hostel? Or both? It's all your call.

Keep in mind the cost of activities as well. Scuba diving excursions, local tours, cooking lessons - they all cost money. This is in addition to living costs. Did you set aside some funds for fun?

Peek the next page for a tool I use for daily budgeting:

Daily Budget Tracker:

This is where that pocket sketch book mentioned in the packlist comes in handy. Every day I'm tracking my expenses, I scribble this down. It doesn't have to look this orderly (mine definitely don't), as long as you can understand it.

Start with your location and the date. Then write T, F, E, H, M in a vertical line down the left of the page.

These stand for the different types of expenses you'll run into on a day-to-day basis, in this case Travel, Food, Entertainment, Housing, and Miscellaneous.

CITY_ _ _____.   DATE___ _ _ _ _

T_____ _ _____ _ ____

F___ _ _____ ____

E____ __ _ _____ __ _

H_ _ ____ __ _____

M___ _____ _____

TOTAL = . _____ __|_ _____

Exchange Rate:____|__ _ ____.

As you spend money in various ways throughout the day, write down the amount you spent in the local currency used. No details. Just a number.

You want to keep this as quick and easy to read as possible.

At the end of the day you'll be able to tally expenses and find your total in the local currency used. Write down the exchange rate and compare it to what you spent that day to find the amount spent in your home currency!

Pro tip: Want to really stretch your budget? One option is to work for your room and board. Take a look at workaway.info to get involved in local businesses and projects.

BANKS.

Banks can make this trip heaven or hell for you. Banks control one main thing that helps your trip flow: money. Being able to communicate with your bank is a must. Will your current bank work for you, or will you need to shop a new one? Start by asking these questions.

Things to find out about your bank:

- Do they reimburse ATM fees? Those $2-6 service charges sure add up overseas.

- Do they have a tool for you to manage your account personally? An online or mobile-app?

- How easy is it to talk to a real person to solve an issue?

- How quick are they to spot and reimburse fraudulent charges?

- What is their maximum withdrawal limit?

- **Best:** Have a personal point of contact at your bank to be your boots on the ground and solve any issues that might arise (s/o Mariana - you the best).

Things your bank needs from you:

- Your general itinerary to unlock access to funds every-where you visit.

Why? Well, your bank is looking out for you by remaining hyper-vigilant of possible fraudulent charges. It may not feel like they're on your side after they cancel your debit card, but know it looks real suspect when cash is sporadically taken out of various ATMs on the other side of the world.

Do yourself and your bank a favor and keep them in the loop.

MONEY TIPS.

Do not carry all your cash in one location.

Have your daily cash ready and accessible, but the reserve wad somewhere safe in your bag, or on your body, that only you know about. This keeps you from whipping stacks of cash out in public places.

Carry two debit cards.

Travel happens. Things are misplaced when shuffling from here to there. Don't be SOL if you leave your primary card somewhere. Hide your secondary access to money for those "doh" moments (happened to me last trip to Thailand).

Check to see if your card is EMV compliant.

Does it have that new-age chip thing? The U.S. apparently didn't get the memo when the rest of the world decided to switch from mag-stripes to EMV chips for payment processing. Your card may not work overseas if you haven't made the switch. Check it out.

Do not use public WiFi to access any personal information.

I've witnessed first hand a hacker pull up bank account information from some unknowing suspect logging on to public WiFi to move around a couple bucks. Kinda scary how easy it was...don't make it easy for 'em.

Cash is king (or queen).

Some vendors don't accept plastic forms of payment, so debit or credit cards are out of the question. Having a few bucks on hand keeps you from standing wide-eyed on the other side of a counter attempting to remember directions to the closest ATM.

"I don't know where I'm going,
but I'm on my way."

- Carl Sagan

TRAVELING WITH OTHERS.

"Some people look for a beautiful place, others make it beautiful."

- Hazrat Inayat Khan

TRAVELING WITH OTHERS.

The biggest impact on the road is made by the people around you. From the highest highs to the lowest lows, people make the experience.

PODS AND SQUADS: DECIDING WHO YOU'LL TRAVEL WITH.

A casual conversation with family and friends about an imaginary trip is easy and fun, and I suggest you do it often. It gets a lot harder when you are talking with your travel pods and squads about where you will **actually** go and what you **will** do.

Harder, but more exciting.

You'll be spending money on these trips, but more importantly you will be spending time. The biggest influence on that time is the people you surround yourself with. Choose carefully who you travel with. Don't make a bad investment.

'Cause let's get real:

Some friends just can't keep up.

Both physically and emotionally, some people aren't ready to hit the road as hard as you want to. Realize that. The last thing you want is to be in the middle of a tough situation and be the only one capable of making decisions. Who will be there for you when shit hits the fan?

You are there to support each other when the going gets tough, to high-five each other when the tough get going, and in all the moments in between. Reinforcements must be strong to be relied upon, so find a sturdy pillar whose head is on straight and wears a smile.

By this I don't mean you and everyone else need to have all your shit together. None of us do. We are growing all the time, and there's nothing like travel to grow you fast (that's one thing I love about it, in case you hadn't noticed). What I do mean is you want to travel with people who are able to be responsible for their own growth and reactions, just as you are.

You don't need to feel responsible for the outcome of someone else's experience.

You have enough to stay aware of.

If you feel someone who wants to travel with you can handle it, then hell ya, go for it. But don't jeopardize your trip feeling you'll have to pull extra weight because little Jeremy tagged along (no disrespect to the Jeremy's out there). You all need to be conscious of your own capabilities, capacities, and comfort levels.

This is your trip, you paid for it, you took the leap. Own it.

Think of it as a group of individuals traveling; you just happen to be doing it together. Everyone knows what they want to get out of the trip, so it is up to them to find a way to fit it in.

All too often I speak to backpackers who are traveling in groups and feel they are missing so much in that location because a majority of the group's interests don't match their own.

To that I say:

There is no obligation to do EVERYTHING together.

What does a relaxing afternoon look like to you? How will you find ways to stretch your comfort zone? What local "something" do you want to learn about? How much are you willing to spend in time and money?

I guarantee answers will differ from person to person. There is no need to limit yourself because of someone else's idea of fun, and you shouldn't feel pressured to spend more than you're comfortable with. You can have it all and there is no disrespect in exploring in your own way.

Don't give up on something you want to do out of politeness. Respect your own dreams enough to do everything you can to realize them. It's not rude to do that. Rudeness only enters the picture when someone delivers their wishes in a rude way or responds to the news rudely.

You can be conscious of people's feelings without being dictated by them.

Take that local cooking class, surf lesson, museum tour, mountain bike ride, and/or anything else that fascinates you. This is your trip, have respect for your travel partner's schedules, but do what you're pulled to do.

If you do peel off just make sure you:

1. Tell everyone what you're doing and where you are.
2. Have a meet-up time and place afterwards, and stick to it no matter what!
3. Have various ways to get ahold of each other (phone #'s, Internet messaging, contact info for activity provider).

Everyone's trip gets ruined if they think you're dead.

Communicate out of respect so they don't send a search party and begin to stress bald in your absence.

COMMUNICATION.

When I'm traveling with groups I encourage everyone to express when they're not comfortable. We all need to be on the same page. Take John Mayer's advice:

> ## "Say what you need to say."

Remember my reference to you all being each other's supporting pillars earlier in this section? Well, you as a human can do something a building can't when it's falling apart - you can talk out the cracks.

And the best way to talk out the cracks is to find what's causing them in the first place. Luckily, I've got a pretty rad tool to do it:

H.A.L.T.

Are you:
Hungry?
Angry?
Lonely?
Tired?

All the above?

HALT reminds us to literally stop. Breathe. Take a look at ourselves and what's causing the tension so we can immediately talk out the cracks, fill the cracks, find stability, and move on.

Hungry? Easy fix. Get a bite to eat. Pack some snacks for the long bus ride. Do what you gotta do to get food.

Angry? What's the issue? Well, consult this flowchart:

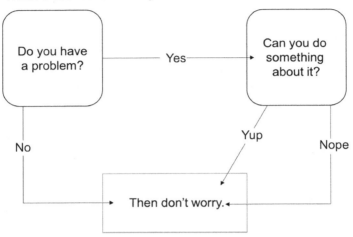

This is where being grateful becomes a beautiful solvent. Look where you are and look at what you're doing. Why waste one moment of it?

Lonely? We all get a little homesick and feel down and alone. Culture shock is real and on occasion getting back into your bed at home seems like it would solve every issue in the world.

Loneliness is a very valid feeling and can throw you into quite a funk. The best way I solve the issue is to find a space to sit down, throw in some headphones, and jam out. Take a walk or find a good book to get the mind elsewhere. Anything that brings you back to ground, cause it's just a phase. Once you're out of the funk, take a look around and breathe. You're pretty courageous for taking such a trip. 'Ain't nobody got time for those vibes on the road.

Tired? I've laid out some sweet napping tips and tricks a couple pages down. I challenge you to give them a shot. Even if you can't handle the issue right away, it's good to at least know what is causing the problem.

You can isolate the issue and manage it later.

If you're traveling with others you get to agree beforehand to **politely** bring up HALT when it's needed. Talking out the cracks isolates the issue, gives you opportunity to solve it, and prevents those pillars from falling.

I promise I'm not talking out of a crack about this one. It was shared with me by a far more experienced traveler (s/o to my sis Theresa!) and has saved so much time and frustration on the road. And, if I'm honest, when I'm home too.

There will be tense moments, and it sure gets a hell of a lot harder to get through them when everyone isn't speaking their truth. Make sure you and all you travel with allow one another to call each other out when experiencing that friction. HALT makes it easier.

It's all out of love.

I know I'd want someone giving me the heads up if I'm making a jackass of myself.

Gain some perspective on your travel partner's perspective.

Below are lists of questions and situations to go over with anyone you're considering embarking on an international excursion with. They'll help you understand your partner's expectations, mindset, and motivation for the trip.

These questions may be awkward at first, but it gets a whole lot harder if they're left unanswered. Plus, I wouldn't want to travel with someone I couldn't have this real conversation with anyway…maybe that's just me.

Start the conversation with this list:

Fill in the blanks, talk through the points, do what you need to do to be on the same page as your travel buddy.

What if:
- we get lost or separated
- one of us gets sick or injured
- we get tired of each other
- we lose our passports
- we want personal time

Expectations:

I want this trip to be _____ (educating, fun, relaxing, etc.).
I want to _____ (learn the language, learn to cook, drink, taste lots of food, meet lots of locals, etc.).

My preferred type of travel is:

- night life
- museums
- adrenaline
- slow and easy
- meet as many people
- low-keyed, slower pace
- budget
- 5-star
- digital nomad

Other info:

I am a (morning, night)_____ person.

I give you permission to _____ me (keep me accountable, call me out when I might be breaking our travel rules, etc.).

When I get stressed, I _____.

When I get angry, I _____.

My budget is $_____/day which includes lodging, food, transportation, activities, misc.

What you should know about my health: _____

_____

_____

This next one is an absolute must.

Emergency contact info:

Name: _____

Phone: _____

Email: _____

You need to know who to get ahold of back home if something goes awry on the road.

MEETING PEOPLE ON THE ROAD.

How will you connect with others on the road?

During a service project?

Over a beer?

During a free diving excursion?

In a Hari Krishna camp on the coast of Peru?

Through agreeing this town is a dump and joking your way through the chaos?

I've met people through all of these outlets.

You're going to meet great people on the road, sometimes more than once.

On my last trip to Thailand I ran into the same dude on three different islands, four separate times, twice in various clubs, once in a restaurant, and mid-beach during the Full Moon Party Christmas day.

We dubbed him "Ratatouille" because of his elusive cartoonish look and his similarity to the main character in that Pixar film. He would appear on the most random occasions. With a smile plastered on his face, his 6'2" skinny frame would come stumbling up to to me. He'd match my expression of awe at the recurring coincidence, and then howl with laughter. We'd end up sharing stories and dance floors until sleep became priority.

We grew to love Ratatouille.

I tell you this because when you're out there, there is no distinct plan - no matter how hard you try. Coincidence will find you and begin not feeling so random.

You'll be asking yourself: "Did that really just happen? What are the chances?"

I encourage you to invite these serendipitous experiences because they open you to possibilities you could never begin to plan.

My family and I call these "Magic and Miracles."

Sometimes moments like these slip by and go unnoticed until you reflect back on the casual choices you made throughout the journey. You can probably think of a time when a seemingly small decision took you on an unexpected adventure. Knowing the power of these "random" decisions will help you continually invite Magic and Miracles.

Just like Ratatouille proved to me again the impact of serendipity, here's an unplanned story that taught me the power of boundaries.

NO-GO-MOE: STORYTIME.

I was teaching English in Turkey as a volunteer (this was my second trip over there) and I came across a guy who gave off bad vibes. We've most likely all run into someone who keeps us a little on edge, and I found one.

From day one, I was curious why he seemed a little off. With both of us being a part of such a rad organization, I convinced myself I must have met him in the wrong context, or it was just in my head.

It wasn't in my head. This guy was strange.

A group of us, including the guy, began traveling around the Turkish countryside to meet the families of students to show the progress these kids were making.

From day one I felt uncomfortable. But why?

This guy insisted we didn't have enough room in the cars for our gear (we did) and told us we needed to leave some of our stuff behind. This went against my gut, but I went along with it anyway to avoid the tension an argument might create.

A couple days into the trip, I realized the full impact of what I'd done.

I'd given this dude complete control over me.

I went against some of my top travel rules:

1. Trust your gut.
2. Don't allow someone to take charge of your schedule.
3. Don't avoid tension for convenience or politeness.

He had total leverage over me and the group by bullying us to leave our stuff behind for what he passed off as our convenience.

We had to stick to his schedule to get our stuff back – and he made this clear.

What followed were days of guilt trips, weird encounters, a random aggressive blow-up in a public restaurant, and ultimately a negative outlook on a whole month spent in that beautiful country. **All because of one man.**

There's more to tell, but this is a prime example of one person having such a huge impact on my experience of a location, and to this day it leaves a bad taste in my mouth.

It was my fault. I'd allowed it to happen. I should have stuck to my rules.

One day I'll be back in Turkey, a little wiser, a little more conscious of my intuition, with a bit tighter grip on my backpack, and I'll enjoy the hell out of it.

An on-going life lesson:

Though it was a shitty experience, this taught me multiple things. I saw my weaknesses and how he managed to manipulate me by saying it would inconvenience the group. I saw the importance of setting limits when gifting my time, and I was reminded again to give my gut a voice - as it was talking from the start.

You will have similar opportunities to apply the "life gives you lemons" scenario.

There will be difficult times - turn them into lemonade by being open to learn.

It may be a little sour and hard to swallow at first, but finding ways to look into your experience as an opportunity to learn about yourself and others allows you to laugh off the jackasses, scam artists, unmotivated booking agents, and anything else that gives some resistance. By doing this, it actually gives you power over them and yourself a chance to grow a little as a person.

It's all part of the experience. It's a massive experiment to see what is relevant and worth your time.

The people, places, and travel-happenings are teachers there to help you figure out what really matters.

Stay aware and smarten up.

"If you don't have a plan, you become part of somebody else's plan."

- Terence McKenna

A GOOD VIBE TRIBE: STORYTIME.

I can still remember sitting at the dinner table on the island of Koh Rong, Cambodia, and looking up from my plate to see a table surrounded by backpackers. Shoeless, sea-showered, and sand-brushed bodies laughed around the dinner table after a day of island exploration. Travelers from Germany to Brazil, Israel to California, South Africa to India - I hadn't known these people in the morning but by night, they were the closest of friends.

I was planning on leaving the next morning, but after finding out that these new friends were hanging around for the week I decided to give it a few more days. Six days later, I didn't know the day of the week, wasn't sure the time of day, was scuba certified on a whim to join a friend from Austria on a couple dives, and was having the best time of my life.

This island was gorgeous, yet looking back I noticed there wasn't anything too special about it before the group had arrived. We were each other's catalysts for daily jungle excursions, sporadic beach hammock naps, snorkeling, and longtail boat sunset cruises. That caused something to click:

90% of a location is made memorable by the the people you share it with.

I may have made that percentage up,
but do I believe there is some truth here.

This applies not only to life on the road, but back home too. You've probably heard, "You're the average of the five people you surround yourself with." Well this never truly sank in until I saw the impact that group of people had on me on a small Cambodian island.

Perk I have homes around the world.

Thanks to those international friends, and others I've met on every trip, my evolution as a "world citizen" gets easier and easier to realize. They know they've got a home in Portland and I know I have one where they live.

As your friends add up, you'll notice your travels revolving around where they are. If you've got a friend in Kenya, you've got a place to stay with someone you enjoy who knows the area and its amazing activities.

Friends are a rad excuse to get going.

GET SHWIFTY.

(Proper Partying)

GET SHWIFTY. (PROPER PARTYING)

Ayooooooooooo! Maybe it's your scene, maybe it's not, but establishing ground rules before you find yourself in a bar or party after a few too many will keep you safe.

This aspect of travel produces some of the best stories, friends, and random encounters in the shortest amount of time. But, a word of wisdom from Ice Cube: "Check yo self before you wreck yo self." There's so much to keep track of that if you don't hold your bearings, it's easy to get lost in the noise. The trick is to stick to the rules you set and don't compromise on any of them.

I repeat: Do not compromise.

I'm not saying this to scare - I'm saying this to save your nights from shady people and circumstances. Set a good foundation for the night and stick to it. If things feel a little off, going home early is a lot better than watching your night, bank account, and sensibilities fall apart.

Clubs and bars will always be there – your health and safety may not.

Note* The clubs and bars I'm mentioning here are absent of coat check or any other form of "order." They play loud music, sell drinks, and usually spill out onto the street, beach, or other surrounding areas.

Pre-game checklist:

- Get a business card with the name, address, and contact info for the place you're staying that night. This is your anchor to get you home after a radical night out.

- Squad. Get a group, or friend, to vibe with for the night (more on this below).

- Minimal bags - none if possible. You don't want to keep track of that on the dance floor.

- Cash only - it is soo easy to:

    1. Feel monetarily confident when you've knocked back a few and ran into some friends (especially if you're quick to the check like I am).

    2. Get your debit card lost or stolen on the dance floor.

    3. Keep a tab open and rack up the drinks.

Again, all this is relative to your budget and partying style, but when I go out I decide on what I want to spend that night and stick to it.

 Pro tip: Remember, if you took a cab there, be sure to save enough for the ride back.

Number 1: Booze buddies

- Go out with a group or partner you trust is out for your best interest. You are there for each other no matter what. You wingman/wingwoman it out, you wingman/wingwoman it home. You are each other's pillars for the night. Help them out in good situations, help them out of bad ones.

- Set a space to meet if separated and exchange multiple ways to get ahold of one another.

- If you leave with someone you met at the club or bar, it is your responsibility to tell your buddy and make sure they're okay with you taking off with that person. Let them know where you're headed and when you'll be back.

- If your buddy is leaving with someone, it's your responsibility to screen said "someone" to get all the info you need to make sure your buddy is safe.

Number 2: Staying in the right space

People are rad, but I choose not to immediately trust them. No matter how nice, generous, attractive they seem, you never know their true intention. And I may be feeling like a mom while saying this, but I can't stress enough how weird people can be. Don't trust 'em.

Doesn't mean you have to be paranoid about people the whole night - just don't put yourself in the space to be taken advantage of.

Shady-vibe avoidance 101.

Creating distance from the wierdos with beardos and the all the in-betweirdos:

- Don't leave your drink unattended. Period. If you leave your drink, it's finished.

- Don't accept alcohol or any other substances from strangers.

- Watch your drink being made behind the bar (I hate to say it, but bartenders aren't always on the straight and narrow).

- Look for your buddy to bail you out of funky situations/ be there for your buddy.

- Leave if your gut says so.

- Saying you want to dance can be your excuse to opt out of anything (no one can argue with dancing).

- "Finding your friend" can also be an excuse to opt out of dancing with someone (anyone who doesn't respect you looking out for your friend isn't looking out for you).

- Do not compromise on your original plans even if they distract from the fun of the night (I'll take short-term inconvenience for long term safety any day).

Number 3: Finding your fill

First, look at your environment. How far are you from your lodging? How comfortable do you feel in this space? Who are you with tonight?

Think about all these factors before deciding how gnarly your dance moves will be due to consumption of alcohol. Look out for yourself and others by monitoring how deep in the drink you get. Don't make your new found friends take care of your drunk ass - find the space where you're having a good time and are still able to take care of yourself. Vibe there.

When it comes to drinking, let self-respect keep you from putting yourself in a scenario where you have to be taken care of by somebody else.

Number 4: Make Moves

Have fun with it. Don't let the fear of what might happen get in the way of what is going to happen. Your vibe attracts your tribe. This last section was simply a list of points to protect yourself, your friends, and your night. Fill in the blanks and let's see what you attract.

CHALLENGE.

Whip out a new dance move and say it's popular in your country. See how many people you can get to join you. Why not?

WHERE YOU SLEEP.

And it won't always be comfy.

WHERE YOU SLEEP.

A traveler's inherent super power becomes the ability to sleep anywhere at anytime.

Airports, grubby hostels, back seats of overnight buses, and outside clubs and karaoke bars (*thud, thud*) are some of the places you may land to grab some sleep. There are many things on the road to interfere with your sleep. Finding the best way to make the world your mattress takes innovation, exploration, and a few insider tips.

Regardless of budget, sometimes circumstance causes you to compromise comfort for convenience. To be ready for spontaneous slumber you're going to want the following:

Gear to have and re-purpose:

Pillow = Clothes' stuffed shirt or beanie, inflatable neck pillow, sweatshirt stuffed into its own hood.

Blanket = Those airplane blankets are pretty nice (just a note, not encouragement to steal), extra jackets and layers.

Eyemask = Any fabric that blocks out adequate amount of light.

Security = Rope, carabineers, shoe string, TSA approved luggage locks.

Earplugs = Real earplugs, headphones, cotton swabs.

Padding/Bedding = Your bags, benches, floors, hammock.

Optional: Traveler sheet - Pretty much a lightweight sleeping bag made of silk, satin, or cotton. A travelers sheet keeps you a fabric's distance away from potentially unwashed hostel bedding and the terrors that may bring. A solid investment for germaphobes.

 Pro tip: Get a hammock. This changes the napping game.

Finding a space:

When locating a place to nap, look for a spot with minimal traffic and use your judgment to assess how easily your stuff is accessible to others. You and your stuff needs to feel safe for a stress-free nap. Stressful naps don't sound any fun - don't subject yourself to one.

Positioning and securing your stuff:

Biggest tip I can give when situating your stuff is to keep it touching you. You want to feel if it moves, is jostled, or grabbed at any time. This is why using your bags as pillows/bedding is best.

Next tip, make a bag blob. By securing all your gear together, you won't constantly be reaching out to make sure all your stuff is within your reach and out of the reach of others.

Final tip, throw a strap around an arm or leg to keep you attached to your bag blob and feeling any movement.

It sounds like quite the process, and an uncomfortable end result, but if you play it right, find the proper angles, the stress-free nap will be worth it.

Getting to sleep:

I can't promise you'll pass out every time. I don't know your napping skills. How tired are you? When I find the secret to spontaneous restful sleep, I'll make sure to keep you in the loop.

What I do know is Jack Johnson, a book, and some cozy layers is a guaranteed K.O. for me.

Focus on slowing and calming your mind. It's a lot harder to do in chaotic places, such as airports or bus terminals, but relaxing music, something to casually apply your mind to, and finding a comfy spot is your best chance at chasing down those Zs.

Happy hunting.

Staying aware during slumber:

You can always catch up on sleep; your only bag of clothes and electronics aren't as easily replaced. Staying aware when you're sleep deprived is an ongoing struggle.

Some tips to keep gear out of the wrong hands while sleeping:

- Carabiner or secure all bags together. This makes it hard to snag just one bag - they have to take them all.

- Now, to keep them from taking it all: Tie or loop a strap around yourself. If the mass of bags is fastened together, you'll feel any movement caused by someone else.

- Mini-carabiner or tie zippers together. This stops the bag from being quickly opened. Making your stuff hard to get into is the best deterrent from theft.

BE A GOOD GUEST.

Wherever I stay I have one main goal:

Get invited back.

I'm willing to go a out of my way to make wherever I stay a little bit better than it was when I arrived. That doesn't mean the place has to be spotless, just respected.

Two key words to being a good guest: Awareness and Gratitude.

1. Stay aware of your stuff and the impact you're having on the room around you.

2. Remain grateful for the space you're in and the bed you have (no matter how shitty - it can always get worse).

These reminders are your tools to navigate the tension you will face when constantly moving between new places. It will be hard to keep your head on straight, but much easier to strap on a smile and laugh about the crazy circumstances you're in. Trust me, it's going to get strange. It will be uncomfortable. It will be challenging to remain positive.

But it will be worth it.

Wherever you stay, either at an AirBnB, a home-stay, a resort, or a hotel, awareness and gratitude will help you keep your head on straight and get you an invitation back.

But there is one lodging situation that needs a little more explaining - where it all goes down and the vibes turn up.

HOSTELS.

hos·tel
/ˈhästl/
noun

An establishment that provides inexpensive food and lodging for a specific group of people, such as students, workers, or travelers.

With such a broad spectrum of hostels, there's no wonder people have had such diverse experiences. Awareness and gratitude remain a constant wherever you stay. Hostels require you to expand both because it's not just about you anymore. Stay aware of yourself and others and be grateful for this space that is much more than just a place to stay.

I've noticed that hostels attract a certain type of traveler - the high-adventure, low-budget explorer.

This creates an interesting atmosphere.

On any given night, you'll find a combo of story-telling artists, musicians, lawyers, gymnasts, police officers, hippies, engineers, photographers, and just about every other character you can imagine. They are all searching for insight and ideas to add to their itineraries, save a couple bucks, and stretch their experience. "Where are you from?" A simple catalyst for conversation and gives hostels that unpredictable element - and you know how I feel about the unpredictable.

Not knowing what's going to happen allows for the possibility of anything to happen.

-cue nervousness and excitement.

I'm a big fan of hostels.

Here are some tips for staying in dorm-style hostels:

Keep your stuff together.

For the safety of your stuff and the convenience of others, try to maintain some order when moving into your bunk. Don't leave bags in the aisle so others have to make an effort to get by. Tuck them under, in a corner, or at the foot of your bed. Your stuff shouldn't be anyone else's problem. Best choice is to use a locker if provided. Keep your gear safe and out of the way so you don't have to stress about it.

Bring earplugs.

Between the possibility of a snorer, the tossing and turning of others at night, and the irregular comings-and-goings of others, earplugs (or headphones for music) help you feel confident in your ability to deter the nightly sounds of a dorm-style hostel.

Get to know those around you.

Who do you have the pleasure of sharing the bunk with? How about the next bunk over? Just another excuse to converse with more people and get a read on the room you're spending the night in. Good or bad vibes? Trust your gut and act accordingly.

No locker - secure the goods.

Thieves still exist in hostels (this applies at night **and** during the day). Secure your passport, cash, and anything else of value by keeping it close. Put it in your pillow, pockets, bag at the head of your bed, etc. Whatever allows you sleep sound that night knowing your valuables are near, do it.

Use those flip-flops for the shower.

Don't put your feet on grubby hostel shower floors - ew.

Be conscious of yourself at night out of respect of others.

This is where I reference the golden rule - do to others what you want done to you. Loud noises, turning on lights, and talking does not sound like an optimal sleeping environment. Promise you won't be that person everyone blames for losing their sleep.

Kitchen Rules:

Most hostels have kitchens for their guests to use. Some ground rules should be set for all those stepping into a shared hostel kitchen.

- Even though the dishes and silverware may be washed - wash them again. You never know how thorough the last person was.
- Don't munch on other people's stuff - involuntary sharing is not caring.
- Leave whatever you use to prep your food as clean as you can (pots, pans, spatulas, whisks, etc.).
- Clean your dishes and silverware right after you're done using them.

CHALLENGE.

Cook a collaborative meal with strangers. Pool your ingredients and chef skills and see what you can make.

Note* Make sure you get the nod of approval before snagging their veggies. Maybe they won't carrot all, but there isn't mushroom for rudeness to turnip in a space like that.

Slow clap

"Let yourself happen."

- Jan Black

TURKEY PART TWO: STORYTIME.

I land in Turkey. This country was absent from my travel radar until invited by a group of musicians to teach English along the west coast. Here was my excuse to begin traveling, and I felt pretty good knowing that excuse involved local service work - which made me feel really good about myself, if you know what I mean.

What I didn't initially see was the impact the locals would have on me. I thought I was the one giving, but soon realized I was receiving much more than I could ever give in that 3-week timespan.

I began seeing there was much more than just me.

I gained perspective as I saw the vastly different circumstances these people were in, yet we shared a similar curiosity and a drive for connection. I gained respect for the tough educational system the kids were in and the way they passionately navigated **and** added to their curriculum. I gained a love of cultural immersion as at times I'd be the only one speaking English in a group of Turkish teens. I often had no clue what was happening.

I was so uncomfortable and I loved it.

This view into what felt like a completely different world intrigued me. The underlying similarities we all shared as humans showed through and nudged us into curious conversation. Most of it was barely comprehensible bi-lingual ramblings ending with simultaneous laughter of confusion. Even as we searched for our next question, in the moments of silence between subjects, I knew we were vibing on each other's presence.

Vibing so hard, I now go out of my way for that local experience every trip I take.

These were just initial interactions with locals. We didn't even start our "service work" yet. But when that time of the trip rolled around, the vibes got exponentially better. Why? Well I found out that my "work" was teaching kids between the age of 4-18 conversational English.

Granted, get stuck with a large group of kids in The States and it'd feel like you're herding cats. But these guys were motivated to learn as much as they could from this white kid with a guitar. I was so different from anyone they'd ever met, they wanted to make the most of our time together, and so did I. It was this crazy mutual fascination we all had for each other that allowed us to have such a rad time and squeeze as much laughter and learning into the days as we could.

THE LOCAL-MOTIVE.

What I gained
through giving.

THE LOCAL-MOTIVE.

It was then I realized what showing up in service did.

Service work brought together two different cultures of people aimed toward solving one goal (in this case teaching and learning English), and that was our icebreaker. It was an immediate foot in the door to the local culture. It was a catalyst for direct interaction and with that exchange we began achieving our set goal together.

While we started making progress on our goal, we celebrated together, and began to bond.

I saw this same process happen in many other volunteer experiences I had after that first Turkey trip. Building homes, cleaning villages of trash, taking care of elephants, playing with orphans, reaping rice, feeding the homeless. It seems to go like this:

Opportunity to help + showing up fully in service
= Cultural understanding
= Perspective and respect
= Thankfulness and gratitude
= Mutual benefit
= New friends
= A need solved.

I'm not saying this is the exact equation for world peace…but I am pointing out the progress that's made when people unite around one common "why" and bring their full value to the table.

If only we could find that "why." *nudge

Now, as you might see, this equation falls apart when one (or more) of the parties aren't really committed to solving that initial goal. Why are you there in the first place? Yes, getting to know and experience a different culture is a valid response, but realize that is the **result** of solving that original issue.

You want to know a culture? Fully give yourself to, and experience, a group of people solving an issue the community needs.

I repeat, solving an issue the community **needs**.

This is the second part of the equation - Opportunity.

Is this a real opportunity to help the community?

Do your research.

Whether you are on a trip sponsored by a non-profit, helping organizations along the way, it's important to ask some questions. How deeply does the organization you're joining impact the locals? Is it solving a deep-rooted problem or just a temporary solution? Is your contribution going where it should?

Stay curious, ask these questions, and stay conscious about your why. This is why I see volunteerism receiving so much flak - some organizations have mixed motives.

Regardless, the difference you can make is to show up and serve well.

Volunteerism can go two ways:

A.   Actively work to solve an issue with the community

B.   Passively watch the issue the community faces.

Please pick A.

"We are called to be
architects of the future,
not its victims."

- R. Buckminster Fuller

Pro tip: You don't need an organization to be your excuse to better the space around you. When I see trash littering a beautiful beach, I take five minutes or so to pick up what I can and throw it away. It betters everyone's view, hopefully encourages others to do the same, and it is a fat THANK YOU to the gorgeous place for being so damn gorgeous.

I now have a local-motive.

Wherever I go I do my best to get involved with the local culture and community; that could look a variety of ways:

- Volunteer/ Service work.
- Ask locals to suggest places to eat or visit.
- Experience cultural events.
- Get to know the history of wherever I am.
- Visit markets and other gathering spaces.
- Learn a few words of the local language.
- Try new foods.
- Check hostel bulletin boards for opportunities or ask your lodging provider how to get involved.

By now, you can see I believe it's about what you give, not what you get.

There's no room for half-hearted acts of service. Go all in.

LIFE IN TRANSIT.

"There was nowhere to go but everywhere,
so just keep rolling under the stars."

- Jack Kerouac

@rileytemp

LIFE IN TRANSIT.

There's something that unlocks when life jumps me between cities I've never been. Surrounded by people I've never met, cultures I've read about, food I've yet to try, and sights to be seen, time slows down. Everything is new. The brain has so much to process that moments are stretched and perspective is changed.

It won't be easy.

When everything around you is foreign - the people, the places, the language – you're going to feel a little uncomfortable. You can no longer blend into the background and go unnoticed. You can't hide yourself in the familiar noise. You stick out. So get comfortable being uncomfortable, cause those okay with sticking out aren't scared to push things, they don't fear instability, they won't settle, and as a result what others consider undoable becomes your done.

Get Going.

ON THE ROAD 101.

From buses to planes, taxis to trains, boats to bikes - there are many different ways to get where you need to go. Keeping an eye on your stuff, an eye on the prices, and an eye on your direction is essential when living on the road.

Safety:

Safety remains a factor to be considered in every decision made on the road.

Is it safe to eat that food? Is it safe to stay on that side of town? Do I really want to walk home this late at night or should I get a cab?

This isn't a matter of pushing your comfort zone, it's a matter of severe importance. If you feel your safety is jeopardized, and you might be put in a vulnerable position, you have every right in the world to leave and get to a safe spot.

There's a big difference in being uncomfortable and genuinely in danger or trouble.

Biggest tool for safety: **Awareness.**

Remain aware of your surroundings.

Remain aware of who's making the decisions.

Remain aware of your ability to remove yourself.

Remain aware of other's intentions.

Stay conscious of conversations you have with people and what info you share with them.

Yes, there's a lot to take in, but pay attention to what will directly affect you. You need to recognize red flags in situations and think through the best ways to exit those scenarios. Think about people's motives to involve you, sell you something, take you somewhere.

What's in it for them? What's in it for you?

If your safety isn't on their agenda, they shouldn't be on yours.

Establish lines to never cross. Those rules will keep you safe.

MY NOPE LIST.

- Arriving in a town at night without transportation and/or lodging set-up.
- Giving my passport to others for longer than a day.
- Accepting anything consumable from anyone I don't know.
- Trusting those I don't know to watch my bags.
- Carrying something for someone else across borders.
- Leaving a lodging provider without its business card or address to get back.
- Carrying large amounts of cash in my main wallet.

WHAT'S ON YOUR NOPE LIST?

THEFT.

Avoiding stickyfingers.

THEFT.

Some say it's inevitable and I will agree you may get fleeced in one way or another. At this point it's damage control. What is most important to you?

Keep it close.

There is no way of remaining attentive at all times. Things will distract you and someone may capitalize on that lack of attention. But there are ways to combat this.

Steal these tips:

Numero Uno: NEVER LEAVE YOUR BAGS UNATTENDED.

This may be common sense but a lot happens on the road - enough to momentarily divert your attention and get your gear swiped. Your stuff is an extension of your body from here on out. Anything you don't want to lose becomes an additional appendage. This also encourages you to pack less.

Don't trust people you don't know to watch your bags.

On a nine-month trip around the world I lost one point-and-shoot camera, a burn cellphone, and 50 bucks. Not too shabby for such a long trip, but I lost those things cause I got lazy. I wasn't thinking when I left a daypack with a tuk-tuk driver for no more than 30 seconds to run into my place to grab something. I compromised out of convenience, and again paid the price. He took what he saw was valuable out of my bag, zipped it back up, and dropped me off before I ever knew things were missing. Cheeky homie.

Be aware when pulling out high-priced goods.

Don't whip out that MacBook Air on a local crowded bus. Don't hang your $2k Canon EOS Mark III camera out the side of your tuk-tuk. Don't walk along a busy road with your iPhone 6s extended in front of you for a quick selfie. By doing so you are announcing to the world "Yo! Check out all this expensive stuff I've got!" The cost of these electronics is more than many locals (depending on country) earn after years of work - if not a lifetime. Don't put yourself, and them, in that scenario. Remain aware of your surroundings.

I've heard so many stories of tourists walking along the side of a road with their smartphones in hand and had them swiped by a local passing on a bike. You can't outrun that motorcycle. You're not getting that phone back. I don't want you to relive this story, so stay aware.

Don't put your bags beneath your seat while in transit.

Another story I've consistently heard from travelers is that putting your stuff under your seat while on a bus, train, boat is an open invitation for Stickyfingers McGee behind you to leisurely sort through your stuff and swipe what's paying for their dinner tonight.

Keep in mind thieves go for the lowest hanging fruit. If you make it easy for them, they'll take what they can. If you make it overtly difficult, they won't try.

Don't allow your gear to be the lowest hanging fruit.

SCAMMED.

It's no fun seeing your bank account take a dip because you've been scammed. It's a sickening feeling and messes up your plans. Being ripped off is something I'd wish upon no-one but those doing the scamming.

I mean what kind of life is supported by capitalizing on the vulnerability of someone else?

Not cool.

To avoid being a hacker's revenue stream:

- Trust your gut if something feels fishy.
- Don't wire money anywhere if not to a traceable and credible source (there's a reason Craigslist warns us about this).
- Don't use public WiFi to manage any banking or financial transactions.

"Experience is a truer guide than
the words of others."

- Leonardo Da Vinci

WHAT WILL YOU MAKE OF YOUR TRIP?

I met people on the road putting together some of the coolest projects from their trip. Here were a few:

- A short video asking people around the world "What makes you smile?" (Shout out to Aslan from the Koh Rong crew.)

- A scrapbook of info docs, train tickets, boarding passes, currencies, maps, and business cards.

- A collection of soil from every continent in the world.

- A book of Polaroid portraits and hand-written stories from friendly foreign encounters.

- A journal of pen drawn memories.

- A multi-cultural dance video.

- A journal signed by people who make an impact on your trip (rad idea Allibobba).

Just trying to get the ideas flowing for you.

What unique something will you make of this trip?

I challenge you to make it inspiring.

_____

_____

_____

(your ideas here^^)

EXTRA CREDIT.

What ways can you take what you've learned on the road and apply it to something to better your community?

Some ideas:

- Coordinate a day of feeding the homeless with friends.
- Start a meet-up for passionate backpackers to encourage and empower others to travel.
- Create an event to highlight the service organizations you worked with.
- Clean a public park of litter.
- Work with Habitat for Humanity. Which, by the way, is a very sweet organization.
- Look for local volunteer meet-ups in your area.

Pumped to hear what comes of this.

This is a way of pushing your comfort zone when things feel a little stagnant – especially after a big trip. It helps me realize things don't have to stay the same and I can always be searching for new experiences to keep lighting me up (a reference to that earlier analogy).

Plus, I get to help people in the process... not too shabby.

Search for different ways to explore what intrigues you, and where you find passion see what you can do to turn it into purpose.

WHAT WILL YOUR TRIP MAKE OF YOU?

WHAT WILL YOUR TRIP MAKE OF YOU?

COMING HOME.

Some say this is the most difficult part of the trip. I agree.

Your return date always seems to sneak up quicker than you thought it would. Those past three weeks on foreign shores came and went, leaving you standing at the airport with a heap of sandy bags and loads of memories. But what now?

Are you going to jump right back into life like you left it? Are you going to switch things up? Has anything changed? You know you're a tad different, but how is that going to mix with the friends and family at home?

From my experience, it will mix beautifully…for the first month. Everyone will be enamored by you having the courage to step off the main track and make the most of life. It's empowering to people. You are a source of inspiration for all those questioning the purpose and direction of their own lives. That's a big responsibility, but don't worry, it'll wear off.

People get distracted quickly.

The initial products of your trip will be the stories you share and the souvenirs you've bought. It will feel good having those to show and remind you of the experience.

But stories fade and souvenirs collect dust.

Three weeks go by, maybe a month, maybe two, and you're back into it. Studying, working, socializing about the same old things. If you're like me, and you've caught the bug, it feels dull, it seems choreographed, it can no longer hold your full attention 'cause you know what's out there. You know it doesn't have to be this way.

This is your matrix moment.

Red or blue pill?

Are you going to put your head down, step back into the routine, and hope for the best? Or are you going to change things to align with your new definition of a rad life?

One tip I can give you to help make that decision is:

That feeling you had on the road, it can be had anywhere.

The mindset of a travel backpacker can be held, it can be applied, it can be used to make your life, and the way you view it, better. Even when you're not on the road. It is a choice you make.

It is a conscious choice to change perspectives.

1. Change your perspective about the power of your decisions.

It's easy to make a choice to change your environment while traveling, it's a lot harder when you're home and have expectations put upon you by others and even yourself. For some odd reason, those expectations tend to mute your ability to make **your** own decisions. Know that.

I make the most I can of every trip. The decisions I make on the road are to better myself and my experience. We forget this at home. We base our choices of self-betterment off the decisions of others in an attempt to validate the direction we are taking.

There is no right way to travel. You need to make your own decisions based on your circumstance (only you can fully understand) and what you're drawn to.

Note* In that last statement, "travel" and "live life" are interchangeable.

2. Change your perspective on the value of your time.

On the road, if someone isn't valuing my time, I know they aren't out for my best interest, and therefore I leave. I don't like wasting my own time, so why let someone else do it for me?

There is a feeling of time slowly slipping away while on your trip, the days fly by, you've prepped so much for this excursion, spent a good chunk of money, now you don't want to waste it. You feel that drive take over on the road. You want to squeeze in as much as you can while you're still here. You're valuing your time in a whole new way.

But what happens to that drive when you get home?

Life's a trip and you've sure spent a lot of time and money prepping for it, so what now?

Find your direction. How?

3. Change your perspective on what is relevant.

The definition of relevant is important to the "*matter at hand.*" What is your matter at hand? What do you value most?

Your job?

The outlook others have on you?

Your happiness?

Living a fulfilling life?

There is no wrong answer here; just know as your values change so do your priorities.

Getting a little sciencey here:

"What you value" is the independent variable, "what is relevant" is the dependent.

So what are your priorities?

If you want to be the most successful at your job, you work hard, and prioritize it before anything else.

If you want to be happy, find what brings you happiness, and make it your number one.

That number one priority becomes your true north. You now get to find unique ways to support what matters to you.

But we get caught up.

We are so quick to apply importance to what others give attention to, thinking it deserves our attention as well.

Let's not get caught up.

We have limited time on this trip. Prioritizing our values keeps our time safe, decisions easier to make, and life always interesting. It stops us from being directed by others toward experiences that don't serve us and even leave us drained.

Remaining aware of what is relevant to our values, and what isn't, is a compass that keeps us stepping in the right direction.

Travel helped me find and dust off that compass. That compass now helps me live my definition of a fulfilling life.

What defines yours?

Find it, share it, and Get Going.

Vibes,

Riley

IT'S ALWAYS BETTER WHEN WE'RE TOGETHER.

(s/o Jack Johnson)

So lets get together.

@RILEYTEMP

this is my insta.

RILEYTEMPLE.COM

this is my website.

THE GOING GOODS.

this is my business.

[thegoinggoods.com]

It would be rad to hear about your upcoming adventures.

THANK YOU.

THE COURAGE VIBE.

An amazing family adventure company that bumps up the adventure of being a family and bucks the myth that families with teens cant have a blast together.

[thecouragevibe.com]

This is my family's business and I am so greatful to each of them for the experiences we've shared, ongoing encouragement, and the drive to make this world a better place. Love you guys.

LIONHEART COFFEE CO.

A good chunk of this book was written on a burnt orange couch in the back of this Beaverton-based coffee shop.

Can't thank ya'll enough for the nitro-cold brews, stories, smiles, and bodacious oasis you've created for so many others and myself. Excited to watch you grow as a socially-conscious company while sharing your love of coffee and good vibes.

FRIENDS WHO DARED TO QUESTION "WHAT IF?"

You helped me write this book. Your curiosity about my backpacking experiences planted the seed for me to write this book and helped me understand in a clearer way the kind of value I want to bring to the world.

This book is for you, and I hope it gives a nudge to keep questioning and exploring, and empowers you with the info you need to continue going.

Let me know what you find.

UNSPLASH.COM

A project created by Crew, Unsplash.com was the source of every gnarly image you've seen in this book.

(Minus that opening shot of me - PC goes to Maddie Black.)

Unsplash.com is updated with 10 Creative Commons Zero photos every 10 days. Because of what y'all created, you helped me bring my book to life and incorporate sweet visual breaks throughout this piece.

You guys are awesome. Looking forward to see what else arises from the Crew studio.

A quick shoutout to all the photographers' images I used as well!

- Cristina Cerda
- Daniel Robert
- Matthew Wiebe
- Didier Weemaels
- Kazuend
- Luke Chesser
- Cynthia del Río
- Daniel Burka
- Ms.Sue Huan
- Farrel Nobel
- Sven Scheuermeier
- Jayakumar Ananthan
- Felix Russell-Saw
- Dmitry Ratushny
- Mickey O'neil
- RhondaK Native Florida Folk Artist
- Erol Ahmed

Thank you again:)

ARTISTS, PHILOSOPHERS, AND THOUGHT LEADERS MENTIONED IN THIS BOOK.

Every individual with a quote in this book has made a profound impact in my life through the living of their own. I aspire to inspire before I expire so I may impact a few to do the same for others.

WHEN GOING
GETS TOUGH.

Sometimes we ebb and then we flow. Life's about the ups and downs, and there is no escaping those lows no matter how hard we try. But your tool to navigate this is the awareness that life does change. You will be back on top. Dory knows -

"Just keep swimming."

And if you need a little bump to keep swimming, I hope the following quote does the trick. It's my personal reminder to get going again.

Thank you, Marianne.

"Our deepest fear is not that we are inadequate. Our deepest fear is that we are powerful beyond measure. It is our light, not our darkness that most frightens us. We ask ourselves, 'Who am I to be brilliant, gorgeous, talented, fabulous?' Actually, who are you not to be? You are a child of God. Your playing small does not serve the world. There is nothing enlightened about shrinking so that other people won't feel insecure around you. We are all meant to shine, as children do. We were born to make manifest the glory of God that is within us. It's not just in some of us; it's in everyone. And as we let our own light shine, we unconsciously give other people permission to do the same. As we are liberated from our own fear, our presence automatically liberates others."

- Marianne Williamson

If you pull anything from this book I hope it is this: you being the truest form of yourself serves the world in a way no one else ever can or will.

Find ways to be more like you, starting now.

GET GOING.

WHAT'S NEXT.

Curating the goods to get you going.

TheGoingGoods.com

CPSIA information can be obtained
at www.ICGtesting.com
Printed in the USA
FSOW04n1052280816
24297FS